Conversations with Good Men

Conversations with Good Men

BETHEL SWIFT

WWW.SWIFTANDSPARROWPRESS.COM
SAN DIEGO, CALIFORNIA

WWW.SWIFTANDSPARROWPRESS.COM

Copyright © 2020 by Bethel Swift

All rights reserved. No part of this publication may be reproduced, stored in a retrieval system, or transmitted, in any form or by any means, electronic, mechanical, photocopying, recording, or otherwise, except for the inclusion of brief quotations in a review, without prior permission in writing from the author or publisher.

Poems in this collection reflect the author's present recollections of conversations, events, and personal experiences over time. In order to maintain anonymity, some characteristics and details—such as names, occupations, physical properties, and places of residence—may have been changed, compressed, or omitted. The author and publisher do not assume and hereby disclaim any liability to any party for any confusion, damage, or loss caused by any changes, composite sketches, or omissions, whether such errors, compressions, or omissions result from mistake or any other cause.

Cover Concept by Bethel Swift
Cover Design by Andreea Arbanas
Interior Design by Navigator Graphics
ISBN • 978-1-7332730-0-8
First Edition Trade Paperback

Publisher's Cataloging-in-Publication Data
Names: Swift, Bethel, author.
Title: Conversations with good men / Bethel Swift.
Description: San Diego, CA: Swift & Sparrow Press, 2020.
Identifiers: LCCN 2019910470 | ISBN 978-1-7332730-0-8
Subjects: LCSH Poetry, American. | Women--Poetry. | Feminism--Poetry. | Man-woman relationships--Poetry. | Love poetry, American. | BISAC POETRY / American / General | POETRY / Women Authors | POETRY / Subjects & Themes / Love & Erotica
Classification: LCC PS3569.W48 2020 | DDC 811.54--dc23

10 9 8 7 6 5 4 3 2 1

DEDICATION

To my writing community
—especially my readers—
for what you bring to these pages.

∼

In loving memory of Mary Bryne Hoffmann.

Contents

Prologue
- 3 • What is Love?

Act I
- 7 • The Artist Takes Herself on a Date
- 9 • Drawn
- 10 • First Kiss
- 12 • Benefits
- 13 • After the Shooting
- 14 • social anxiety attends the party
- 16 • Unforgettable
- 17 • Questions

Intermission
- 21 • My Father on Gchat
- 22 • Buying My First Car & So I Bring You Along
- 24 • Mindful Descent
- 25 • Lessons from My Father
- 26 • Undiagnosed

Act 2
- 31 • Perspectives
- 32 • Once Upon a Springtime
- 34 • Merits
- 36 • DTR with an HSP
- 37 • Fated Female Intuition
- 38 • Break-Up Bread
- 40 • Sentiment
- 41 • Cyclone Courtship

Intermission
- 45 • A Single Tale
- 46 • Dear Adam
- 47 • Prayerspeak
- 48 • Maiden's Prayer
- 49 • Bless Me Father for I Have Sinned

Act 3
- 53 • Roulette
- 54 • Kamikaze Kisser
- 55 • Consumed
- 56 • Consent
- 59 • Potpourri Rain
- 62 • Truth Be Told
- 63 • Lycanthrope
- 64 • Lycanthrope [Spanish Version]

Epilogue
- 69 • Couples at the Harold Washington Cultural Center

Endnotes

Acknowledgments

About the Author

Prologue

What is Love?

Chicago winter
atop old Ramova's roof
pigeons neck in pairs

ACT 1

The Artist Takes Herself on a Date

And I who looked for only God, found thee!
—Elizabeth Barrett Browning, "Sonnet XXVII"

Was it pure chance
or a Freudian slip?

This night I chose to wear
the same black & blue
deep-pocketed dress,
woe-woven scarf,
glossed ebony mary jane's,
(push up bra & unlucky
lace-trimmed underwear)
to the Cadillac Palace—
the theatre where we saw
The Book of Mormon.

There, your interest in me
waned, even as my love for you
began, displacing my faith in God
& man, their co-authored books,
letters, & works of fiction.

Tonight, I lean in to no one,
as I watch dancers
whose sheathed torsos
heaving between sets

remind me
to release my held breath.

Still holding all else in:
memories of your smile,
your spicy aftershave,
your neatly ironed slacks,
your surprised laughter,
guiding hand at my back,
& your eyes—warm stars
in my long dark night.

Drawn

"This couch is uncomfortable,"
you said with an easy smile.

& it surprised me how I let you
lead me to your bedroom, as if I
were following doctor's orders;
a simple "hop up" & there I was:

in your bed,
in your arms.

First Kiss

Your kiss opened like a bloom:

>a butterfly blessing on each eyelid,
>a feather-like tweak of my button nose,
>a warm hand, gently tilting my chin,
>like a slow dance to a sweet song
>—then the tender brush of barely touching lips.

But it quickly grew

>hungry

>>intense

>>>a *man's* man of a kiss.

An ocean wave pulling me out farther than I knew how to swim,
your tongue asking questions faster than mine could answer,
hands roaming the hills and valleys of me as paint over a canvas.

To you, this *chummi*, an open-ended invitation
—a chance you take to get lucky with a friend.

To me, the elation of *he likes me back!*
and the gut punch of *but not enough.*

So I apologize.
And break it off, because
I believe I'm supposed to.

Mother always said, "Never lead them on."
Dad was faithful to warn:
"Men want one thing and *only* one."

But you don't take what isn't yours,
and I don't give permission.

We remain friends who give each other
awkward hugs and make empty promises
to keep in touch—even when worlds away.

What my parents didn't know to say:
the good guys who only *want* to be bad,
when faced with hope-filled eyes,
will eventually confess:

"I don't want anything serious."

So I learn that
from your kiss.

Benefits

I regret my regret
for not being all-in with the moment,
with being yours *just in that moment*—
temporarily trusting the leading of desire,
letting temptation top that dogged longing
for forever.

For lasting love
can't be guaranteed anyway,
can't be securely sealed away

    as moments,

        as memories

(of sure embraces and first dances
long kisses and deep blushes).

Benefits all
tinged now
with knowing …

I couldn't live with myself
being only
your dirty little secret.

After the Shooting

It's a beautiful day in Bridgeport
when we meet up for brunch.

I'm missing his neighborhood,
sick of defending my own Back of the Yards.

He listens with concerned frown,
tumbleweed locks spilling over a creased brow,
dark eyes almost always dancing, but quiet now,
as I tell him about the drive-by shooting last night.

He sighs, shakes that silly yet practical head, says,
"You should invest in a bulletproof vest!"

I can't help but smile. Laugh off longing—
and the absurdity of it all—lay a playful hand
on his chest, thinking: *Without you, my love,
I don't even square up—I just bare my breast.*

SOCIAL ANXIETY ATTENDS THE PARTY

*And, looking on myself, I seemed not one
For such man's love!*
　　—Elizabeth Barrett Browning, "Sonnet XXXII"

i come bearing cake,
place tray on table laden with curries & samosas,
blush at effusive praise for its store-bought design,
omit it was i who lovingly placed the border on:
one hundred chocolate chip kisses, each a teardrop
—a wish to be enough.

"you are a person who is always there,"
he says to me, as a way of saying hello.
meaning, i suppose, that a wallflower
contributes something—if only as decor.

i shelter in his shadow,
reach, not rise, to press perspiring palms
& give gentle hugs.

music, dance, stories, laughter—
this is my tribe but i don't speak the language;
this is my language but i don't speak
—my words form only on paper.

i warm to his sun
but not fully,
& never in time,
smile dying on my lips
before it reaches my eyes.

Unforgettable

I rarely reminisce about your kiss
—my first & our last—
but with every clap of thunder,
firecracker, or car backfire—
I am reminded of your hug.

My PTSD had never known
such safety. Such love.

QUESTIONS[1]

Where have you been, Sir?

And,

how long will you be

... staying?

---

[1] I'll have for (but won't ask of) the next ~~seemingly sweet soulmate, skeptical spiritual pilgrim, honest to God gentle~~man I mistake as mine.

Intermission

My Father on Gchat

"Love you!"
I typed, adding an emoticon smile.

He replied,
"I hate those ugly little creatures!"

BUYING MY FIRST CAR & SO I BRING YOU ALONG

The young salesman
with the slicked-back hair
takes my hand, envelops
it in both of his, pleading
with me to *just trust him*.

I look to you for backup.

You're embarrassed,
but which bothers you more?
Not knowing?
(What *is* a good deal on a service plan?)
Or me not trusting?
(He *seems* like a good man.)

See, there it is again:
I'm always wanting you
to pull out a shotgun,
lay it across your knees,
stare down my enemies
—but that isn't your way.

You say it shouldn't be mine,
but you planted me in the ghetto
in bloodied ground, amid siren songs.

From each rose grown in the concrete
—a thousand thorns.

I fight to the death—an alley cat.
Never at peace. Never at home.

Mindful Descent

He said to me, "You know
I get down sometimes,
but then I get back up.
You *always* seem down."

I should remind my father
that it isn't polite to brag.
(Downright dangerous to address
a slinky with how things *seem*.)

Instead, I offer a sad smile, as I know
that gravity affects even a yo-yo.

When I am only halfway up,
hesitating at the edge of the stair,
I may be neither down nor up
but I am completely *there*.

Lessons from My Father

"Poor planning on your part,"
I remember you used to say,
"... does not constitute
an emergency on mine."

So I'd ponder over plans
B through Z in terror,
fearing if it all went to shit,
no one would be there
holding on the other line.

But I also remember
you driving me to the ER
in the middle of the night;
how you kept glancing back at me,
our faces blanched in the moonlight.

Your silent sympathy,
a sermon in love—
only the wisest fathers
learn not to preach.

Undiagnosed

The doctor gave you
a clean bill of health.

"So, I guess I'm fine," you said,
flopping into an armchair to rest,
before falling to your knees again
just trying to rise up to a stand.

You've been falling for years:
for my mother's revisionist history;
through the walls of the very house you built
to her plans; into old habits, of losing
your temper (yelling at us, yelling at her)
and then down, down, down again
into long silences heavy with guilt,
hoarded with generations of pain.

And still you rise
with the anxious look
of one who has tried,
too hard, for too long
—carried too many burdens
to lay at the foot of the cross.

ACT II

Perspectives

Is that your glass there?
And may I ask, how *you* see it?
Half-gone or nearly full of purpose?

Do the leaves, I wonder,
blush crimson with love for autumn?
Or fall trembling for fear of winter?

I should garden, buy a cactus, or get a cat;
take up violin, learn to tango, attempt to sketch;
"look after orphans and widows in their distress..."

Most days, though, it seems too much
just keeping myself alive and kicking
(high maintenance spine & sourpuss stomach!)

If I had another chance to kiss his lips
I would never stop.
If I had another chance to hold his hand
I would never let go.
If I could stop watching hourglass sands
—I would.

Once Upon a Springtime

First date: you held my hand
and it felt like you always had.

Second date: you questioned,
"How good are you at kissing?"
and I wished I was the best.

Third date: you cupped my breast,
wondered at it being more than a handful,
told me it was a gift.

Four things that endear me to you:
(five that make me forget
how little we have in common)

when you forget a word in English
and say "this one" instead;

when you hover above me with the strength I need
staring deep into my eyes with all of your longing and laughter;

when I can stroke your hair and cradle your head
in my arms or on my breasts,
or lie there with you, resting my head upon your chest;

when you lay your hand on my thigh with soft caress,
thumb tapping out peace signals to calm
my ever-present anxiousness.

And I think: *Body, breathe! Heart, this time it might be okay!*
Soul, perhaps this is your mate? Your homeland address?

Then your firm embrace
negates the need for words of comfort;
and when you do speak again,
you assure me how well I fit into your plans.

It is then, I must remind you
(I must remind myself!)
how easy it is to fall for you.

But oh, my dear,
I am so tired.

So tired of falling

and never being

        caught.

Merits

> . . . *givers of such gifts as mine are, must*
> *Be counted with the ungenerous . . .*
> —Elizabeth Barrett Browning, "Sonnet IX"

i dim in your presence,

fearing i will take too much from You—

Your space,

    valuable time,

        healing touch,

            eyes that warm me through.

Your energy,

    attentive ears,

        musical laughter,

            perennially positive point-of-view.

& what if, when i find that i do,

i still have no worthwhile gift for You?

for of what benefit are these boons?

        strength, to a man who shows no fear—

        comfort, to a man who knows no tears—

        empathy, to a man who feels no pain—

        help, to a man who shows no strain—

such gifts I offer, in truth, but in vain.

DTR WITH AN HSP[2]

Am I asking for too much
too soon?

Am I asking for too little
too late?

Am I overthinking all of this
when you were only seeking
"someone who doesn't take
life too seriously" to date?

Because, my dear, I do.

& if I have to change
to change your mind
then I was never yours
& you were never mine.

---

2   Defining the Relationship with a Highly Sensitive Person

Fated Female Intuition

From the beginning I thought
he should be with the kind of woman
who would pressure him to get his car washed;
who on date nights, would make him make the drive to pick her up;
who, if threatening to break up, would force him to give more
than mansplained philosophical reasons why they should not.
A sophisticated lady with class enough to match his caste
who'd want the La Jolla estate, the BMW, the yacht . . .
The whole time we dated—I felt I was in her spot.

BREAK-UP BREAD

I bake you a loaf of banana bread
the night I break us up.

Something sweet and good
like you say I am.

Something that can't be
overthought, like I always do.

Something I can give,
in place of myself, to you.

Because I don't know how else to declare love
and still break things off.

Because you *are* a magic man,
and maybe, if I were younger, I *could*
let you mold me with those magic hands.

But your spell is wearing off,
(mine, over you, never took)
and the last thing to go
is your enchanting touch.

I am slowly, anxiously, drifting
away from you—and myself.

It's true, you awakened the woman within.
And if I close my eyes, I am back there again:
shivering as your fingertips brush my skin,
hands running through my hair, like a whisper,
"Where do you like me to kiss you better?"

But, you don't believe lovers
can be friends,
and I need that too.
I need so much from you.

When I say, "I know you don't love me yet."
(I mean: *I already love you.*)
You respond with, "Aww . . ."
(And mean: *True.*)

So now this bread is a buffer
between our parting and your indifference.
You accept my offering with one suggestion:
"Walnuts would make it better."

Sentiment

I'm trying to "stay amazing"
like you told me to
but I never felt I *was* amazing
when I was with you.

Cyclone Courtship

        Turned "the One" off by not being willing.

        Turned the next down for not being "the One."

Turned a new leaf, found it already browning.

    Turned to run, found you were standing down.

        You see, I am stronger than my cravings.

          (closer to caving under yours.)

            Comparing mice to men to boys

                  only fills columns in tables

            cathartic discarding, disregarding . . .

Turned down this last, grinning glass,

        for fighting crickets,

        for having fun;

           it seemed so cruel.

            I like their

                  sound.

Intermission

A Single Tale

They say that I'm the picky one.
Who laughs at men as circus clowns.
Who sees their acts, but turns them down.
Then walks on stilts—tall and alone.

They want to see me settle down.
(What to settle, beyond the score?)
They try to make my thinking sound.
(What—sound as sleep—on peaceful shore?)

They say that it is best that I—
When drained from kissing dreary skies,
When weary wearing pride's disguise—
Then choose one to cheer. To chastise.

To comfort heart with loving lies.

Why then shame Adam and blame Eve?
Where they sought knowledge from a tree;

Untethered—how I aim to be.

Dear Adam

> . . . *all women secretly desire to be sacrifices;*
> *they long to be the 'chosen one'.*
> —Jenny Boully, "Footnote 131"

Are you as afraid for God
to remove a single rib
as I am to remain so gifted
to be yet unruled, unwed?

Is it your devotion to our Lord,
which keeps you blind to mine?
There exists—on this earth—no
uncursed woman, you will find.

Recall, it was our Lord God spoke,
"It is not good for the man to be
alone." And He, who kept his vow
to "make a helper suitable for him."

Do you find me so unsuitable
as to eschew me as a shrew?
To shame me merely for longing to belong
as dear as name, as flesh, as bone to you?

Prayerspeak

Lately,
I've been viewing God
as a baby-bearing tree
& thinking maybe,
if I could just shake Him,
he would drop one down to me.
But I wouldn't want the child to get hurt
in the fall which I guess would really be my fall . . .
Anyway,
Heaven is a long way to climb to ask—
with sackcloth & ash—to end this fast & they say,
God doesn't give us our idols, anyway.
So, I guess . . .
No?

Maiden's Prayer

Lord, if I have a husband, listen,
Will you let him know I care?
Even now, I somehow miss him.
(And wish I knew for sure, he was there.)

Lord, will you send a breath of wind to kiss him?
Might sun rays and ocean waves caress his hair?
And when he's feeling down, Lord bless him,
Let the rain be to him my imperfect prayer.

And Lord, if we should meet and marry,
Ah, that we could share so many years!
And while we make each other merry,
Make up for all our tears and fears.

May we always love and listen,
May we ever kiss and forgive,
May we be good to our children,
And thus, happily, together live.

BLESS ME FATHER FOR *I* HAVE SINNED

becoming fat, feminist, forthright,
& free.

Yet I still dance,
live & learn, laugh & love,
asking permission only of me.

ACT III

Roulette

> We don't roll this die
> > of danger equally.

> Men fear for their pride;
> > women, their lives.

> I have been lucky, here,
> > in my heartbreak.

> The hope? To be loved
> > —sexy *and* safe.

Kamikaze Kisser

(After Mother Goose)

Georgie Porgie goes by good name *Don Juan*.
He knows how to make a female friend run.

Harmless, boyish, charming, chuckling chum,
He steals furtive glances all evening long;
Tugs his cap nervously, yet leaves it on;
Keeps his hands neutral while walking along.

But when she offers him a goodnight hug—
Swivels his head to plant a quick one on!

Consumed

"I think..."

said the praying mantis
to her mate, during sex,

"...not *everyone* tries
their very best."

Consent

1.
Go, girl,
into the hills,
but mourn betrayal
—not your chastity.

2.
You can't always tell
who is safe to meet at the well.

I've watered camels,
kissed frogs,
acquired allergies to earrings,
nose rings, and bangles.

But, having left the fold voluntarily,
there is no one to bring me back at Easter.

3.
Esau traded his birthright for sustenance.
I traded my virginity for a few hours sleep.
To be fair, it seemed to me, I had no choice.
But whose truth shall we record?

Whose seal? Whose staff? Whose cord?

The ancients' stories never describe the taste:
Jacob savoring his own stew,

Amnon, his sister's bread . . .
You, hands sticky from my grapes
—stolen honey worth a loved one's disgrace?

4.
What *is* mentioned is resentment:
the hatred that overcomes affection.
At its best, a slipshod apology offered
like a cheap token, for lust eclipsing trust.

5.
You asked afterwards, "Do you hate me?"

Shall I divide my loved ones,
send them ahead in two companies?

And I, again, fell silent as a prayer,
offering cool comfort to your repentance,
a sort of last rites performance.

6.
Maybe it all boils down to mandrakes & desire.
Man has "needs." Woman must preserve the family line.
Man demands a body—his, hers, yours, or mine,
Lot's daughters, David's lovers, a nameless Levite's concubine
to be used to shame a tribe, divide a nation, start a war—
into which he can pour out his guilt, as the gods do their wrath.

7.
Just lie there like a good girl, Dinah, be a sinner in my hands.

You have already been struck blind to my worth.
Deaf to my voice. I, dumb, realizing how mistaken
I was about you. About me. About how, so calmly,
it has come to this – taking.

"No, my brother, do not force me!"

POTPOURRI RAIN

Four dozen
long-stemmed, de-thorned,
blood-red roses cut down
for you to apologize
without words.

Breathing in their fragrance,
I recall a magic formula
for happy relationships,
count ten blessings
for each complaint.

Mathematically speaking, I am supposed to save us:

>   for Isabelle, the tiny shell you brought back
>   for me from flight school;

>   for the tupperware full of chocolate kiss sugar cookies
>   I baked for your return;

>   for that ugly oversized "I Can Fly" t-shirt
>   you thought I might like for a nightgown;

>   for the blisters I earned hunting with you
>   for that one "gnarly" bridge downtown;

for your fear of snakes, my bravery at karaoke,
    & our mutual impotence at shuffleboard;

for your skill at piloting the Romeo & Juliet
    & yet not being able to close its door;

for those photos you weren't ready for me to take
    & the kisses I wasn't ready to give;

for the too-much, too-soon thrill of you claiming me
    by naming me your *Jaan*;

& now, for these, *with all your love.*

But what of the sanctity
of letting one's yes be yes
—their no, no?

Trust is a fickle thing,
a fragile thing,
a patternless puzzle of a thing
with no aeronautical charts known to men
& not enough parachutes for women.

The morning after things fell apart,
I hugged your Buddha belly to me.
Your shoulders, slumped in defeat,
knowing you'd knowingly hurt me.
We agreed in silence.

In the following days you tried
to cheer us up,
joking about chastity belts,
blaming beer
& maybe, just a little bit
—*ladki beautiful?*[3]

You promise next time to be you:
sincere, kind, patient, & gentle.

Tonight, I light a candle,
your peace offering pressed between my palms
& make "next time" promises to you:

    to rise up in raiment robes of Draupadi,
        thwarting your attempts, with my endless dignity;

    to leave & look back, only to laugh last,
        shedding no tears when the final bloom dies;

    to crush & release it as fragrant ashes,
        falling, like foolish Icarus, from the sky.

---

[3]   the beautiful girl

Truth Be Told

    I wasn't impossible to read.
    You're not impossible to write.
    It wasn't a misunderstanding.
    It was date rape.

LYCANTHROPE

"But anyone who would do *that*,"
he said.
"... is an *animal!*"

"Do you think *I* am an animal?"

I answer slow,
deliberate as sex with a corpse,
a hand over a mouth,
a yes, over a—

No.

"No, I don't think you are an animal."
But, are you a shapeshifter?

Because ...

he was.

Lycanthrope [Spanish Version]

"¡Pero cualquiera que hiciera *eso*,"
él dijo.
"... es un *animal!*"

"¿Crees que soy *un* animal?"

Respondo lentamente
y deliberadamente
como teniendo sexo con un cadáver,
una mano tapando una boca,
un "sí" sobre un—

No.

"No pienso que seas un animal."
¿Pero, eres un cambiaformas?

Porque ...

él lo era.

Epilogue

COUPLES AT THE HAROLD WASHINGTON CULTURAL CENTER

This time, when I fall in love, let it be more than a mirage.
This time may I have a poker face but no need to put it on.
This time let it be both partners awakening—not only one
—gliding, smooth as steppers' shadows, moving in unison,
fogging up ballroom windows with their winter passion.

Endnotes

The Artist Takes Herself on a Date - Title is a nod to The Artist's Way by Julia Cameron. Epigraph is taken from "XXVII" of Elizabeth Barrett Browning's *Sonnets From The Portuguese*.

First Kiss - Chummi is "Kiss" in Hindi.

After the Shooting - Bridgeport and Back of the Yards are both neighborhoods in Chicago. "Square up" is slang for getting into a fighting stance. Bearing one's breast is an older idiom for exposing oneself in a vulnerable unguarded state.

social anxiety attends the party - Epigraph is taken from "XXXII" of Elizabeth Barrett Browning's *Sonnets From The Portuguese*.

My Father on Gchat - Gchat is a now defunct instant messaging service from Google.

Buying My First Car & So I Bring You Along
 —References Tupac Shakur's "The Rose That Grew from Concrete" the title poem in a collection of 2Pac's poetry (published posthumously).
 —"Siren songs" references the human-like beings from Greek mythology who sing hypnotizingly haunting songs to lure sailors to their deaths.

Lessons from My Father - The last two lines are a loose "Papa Don't Preach" Madonna reference from her album *True Blue*.

Undiagnosed - The final stanza references the book *And Still I Rise* by acclaimed author Maya Angelou.

Perspectives - The partial quote is from James 1:27 (NIV).

Merits - Epigraph is taken from "IX" of Elizabeth Barrett Browning's *Sonnets From The Portuguese*.

DTR with an HSP - (Defining the Relationship with a Highly Sensitive Person) - The quote is pulled from many a male's online dating profile.

Break-Up Bread - The sixth stanza contains a reference to the song "Magic Man" by Heart.

Cyclone Courtship - Inspired by the lyrics to "If I Didn't Know Any Better" from the album *Lonely Runs Both Ways* by Alison Krauss & Union Station. Also referenced is John Steinbeck's *Of Mice and Men*.

Dear Adam: Epigraph is taken from "Footnote 131" in *The Body: An Essay* by Jenny Boully. Both quotes are from Genesis 2:18 (NIV).

Bless Me Father for I have Sinned - There is a movement within the Body Positive community to reclaim the word "fat" and this poem is my way of doing that. The usage of the term in this poem is descriptive, not derogatory. The title is doing the work of acknowledging the social stigma and shame—especially in the evangelical Christian world—that words like "feminist" or "fat" still carry.

Roulette - The second stanza references poet and activist Margaret Atwood's statement, as paraphrased in Gavin de Becker's *The Gift of Fear*, "Men are afraid that women will laugh at them. Women are afraid that men will kill them."

Consent - References listed below by stanza:
  —References for #1 are: "Jephthah's Vow and Victory" & "Jephthah's Daughter" from Judges 11:29-40 (NKJV).
  —References for #2 are: "Isaac and Rebekah" Genesis 24 (NIV); "The Princess & the Frog" fairy tale; "Jesus the True Shepherd", "Jesus the Good Shepherd", and "The Shepherd Knows His Sheep" from John 10:1-30 (NKJV); "Dovey's Story" in Peter Balakian's memoir *Black Dog of Fate*, as quoted here: " . . . I could see my mother's face as it floated on the white lace of our dining table. *She was saying to me: Let them take you, let them take you, we will bring you back at Easter.*"
  —References for #s 3 & 4 are: "Jacob and Esau" Genesis 25:29-34 (NIV); "Judah and Tamar" Genesis 38 (NIV); "Amnon and Tamar" 2 Samuel 13 (NIV); "grape" is a term for "gray area" rape coined by comedian Amy Schumer.
  —Reference for #5 is "Jacob Prepares to Meet Esau" Genesis 32:1-21 (NKJV).
  —References for #6: "Jacob's Children" Genesis 29:31-30:24 (NIV); "Sodom and Gomorrah Destroyed" and "Lot's Daughters" Genesis 19 (NIV); "The Advice of Ahithophel and Hushai" 2 Samuel 16:15-23 (NIV); "A Levite and His Concubine" and "The Israelites Punish the Benjamites" Judges 19 and 20 (NIV)
  —References for #7: "Sinners in the Hands of an Angry God" is a famous sermon originally delivered by Jonathan Edwards; "Dinah and the Shechemites" Genesis 34 (NIV); and "Amnon and Tamar" again, but 2 Samuel 13:12 (NKJV) specifically.

Potpourri Rain - References listed in order of appearance:
  —The "magic formula" is taken from "Day 3 Magical Relationships" in the book *The Magic* by Rhonda Byrne.
  —"Gnarly" is a word originating in California which carries a wide range of meaning from "dangerous" or "intense" to "cool".

—*Jaan* is a term of Sanskrit/Urdu roots that translates to "life" and is a term of endearment for a loved one.

—The concept of letting one's yes mean yes and their no, no is discussed—in the context of the immorality of taking oaths—in Matthew 5:37 and James 5:12 (NKJV).

—The phrase "things fell apart" is a reference to *Things Fall Apart*, a novel by Chinua Achebe.

—"ladki beautiful" loosely references the song "Kar Gayi Chull" from the Kapoor & Son's film soundtrack.

—Draupadi is one of the most significant females in the *Mahābhārata* (one of the two major epics of Hindu Mythology from ancient India, the other being the Rāmāyana). The tale of her neverending saree takes place when one of Draupadi's husbands (the five Pandavas) wagers her in a bet and loses, effectively making Draupadi a slave to the Kauravas. When an attempt to disrobe and shame her was made in court, Draupadi prayed to Krishna. No matter how many layers of her saree were removed, more remained.

—Icarus, son of inventor Daedalus, flew too close to the sun (on wings his father had made from wax, wood, and feathers) and fell to his death in a famous Greek myth.

Lycanthrope - The phrase "sex with a corpse" refers to the derogatory slang terms "dead fish"/"dead lay"/"dead fuck" used to describe (primarily) females who do not actively participate in the act of penetrative sexual intercourse. Popular culture views this as "laziness" on the female's part for "making the man do all the work" when it is likely a sign of her discomfort—be it hesitation to engage in a specific act with a specific person at a specific time, or due to physical pain or emotional trauma from past or present abuse.

Acknowledgments

My heartfelt gratitude goes out to:

- Open Mic poetry community leaders in San Diego and Chicago for allowing me to read my work in front of their audiences.
- *Armenian Poetry Project, Haiku Journal,* and *Expressions from Englewood* for publishing my work. An earlier version of "A Single Tale" appeared in Vol VII of EFE.
- Proofreader Sandra de Helen (*Desire Returns for a Visit, All this Remains to be Discovered*)
- Copy Editor Kristina Marie Darling (*Look to Your Left: The Poetics of Spectacle, Dark Horse: Poems, Scorched Altar: Selected Poems & Stories 2007-2014*)
- AWP Writer to Writer Mentor: Sandy Coomer (*Available Light, Rivers Within Us, The Presence of Absence*)
- Sensitivity Read/Translation Help: Angika Basant, Briselda Casimero, Rocío Díaz, Angelica González, Sabah Kadri, Christine Marquez, Saurin Mehta, Minu Mittal, Jesús Muñoz, Hector Solis, and Cynthia Valdez.
- Beta Readers: Jenna Benson, Deborah Jang (*Float True*), Sonya Kamell, Emily Peterson and all the members of both of my former Right Alice Writes Critique Groups (Chicago-based and online).
- Publishing Advice: Leslie Browning (Homebound Publications), Robin Cutler (Ingram Spark), Joanna Penn (The Creative Penn Podcast, Website, and Blog), Teri Rider (Top Reads Publishing), Jeniffer Thompson (Monkey C Media), Brooke Warner, (She Writes Press) as well as the IBPA (Independent Book Publishers Association) and PWSD (Publishers and Writers of San Diego).
- Logo Design: Sarah Swift Designs.

About the Author

Bethel Swift is a San Diego based author/publisher, mixed-media visual artist, speaker, workshop instructor, and professional home organizer. Her poetry has been published in *Armenian Poetry Project, Haiku Journal, San Diego Poetry Annual,* and *Expressions from Englewood* as well as exhibited at her alma mater Columbia College Chicago. In 2020, she founded her publishing company and published *Conversations with Good Men,* (Swift & Sparrow Press) in print, ebook, and audiobook after attending IBPA (Independent Book Publishers Association) Pub U Conferences in 2018 and 2019. Bethel served on the Board of the former SDMWA (San Diego Memoir Writers Association which is now the International Memoir Writers Association) for two years. In 2017, she was the recipient of an AWP (Association of Writers and Writing Programs) Writer to Writer Mentorship with poet Sandy Coomer (*Available Light*) and a panelist at their annual Conference & Bookfair in 2020. Prior to that, Bethel studied poetry under Kristina Marie Darling (*Dark Horse*) and Larry Sawyer (*Vertigo Diary*) at the Chicago School of Poetics and with Martha Vertreace-Doody (*Glacier Fire*) at Kennedy-King College. She earned her degree in journalism from Columbia College Chicago (in 2007) and her journalistic features, interviews, reviews, and opinion pieces have appeared in multiple print and web publications. Swift and Sparrow Press maintains an active presence in the local author scene including book festivals and local writer events. For more information on Bethel, please visit her website bethelswift.com.

www.ingramcontent.com/pod-product-compliance
Lightning Source LLC
Chambersburg PA
CBHW021129080526
44587CB00012B/1204